J
523.
4
GRA

SPACE

PLANETS FAR FROM EARTH

Ian Graham

Smart Apple Media

Published by Smart Apple Media,
an imprint of Black Rabbit Books
P.O. Box 3263, Mankato, Minnesota, 56002
www.blackrabbitbooks.com

U.S. publication copyright © 2015 Smart Apple Media. International copyright reserved in all countries. No part of this book may be reproduced in any form without written permission from the publisher.

Designed by Guy Callaby
Edited by Mary-Jane Wilkins

Cataloging-in-Publication Data is available from the Library of Congress

ISBN 978-1-62588-211-0

Picture acknowledgements
t = top, b = bottom, l = left, r = right
title page Aleksandar Vozarevic;
2-3 CoreyFord; 4-5 Dimitar Marinov/all Thinkstock; 5b NASA, ESA, H. Weaver (JHUAPL), A. Stern (SwRI), and the HST Pluto Companion Search Team;
6 CVADRAT; 7 Sabino Parente; 8 Stephen Girimont; 9 patrimonio designs ltd;
10-11 Elenarts/all Shutterstock; 12 Digital Vision/Thinkstock; 13 FomaA/Shutterstock;
14 Ablestock.com/Thinkstock; 15 Byron W.Moore/Shutterstock; 16 Lars Lentz;
17 Jason Reed/both Thinkstock; 18 JULIAN BAUM/SCIENCE PHOTO LIBRARY;
19 Stocktrek Images; 20 Elenarts;
21 Stocktrek Images/all Thinkstock
Cover tl MarcelClemens/Shutterstock;
tr Digital Vision; br MarcelC; bl Martin Adams/all Thinkstock

Printed in China

DAD0057
032014
9 8 7 6 5 4 3 2 1

Contents

The far planets	4
Jupiter	6
Exploring Jupiter	8
Saturn	10
Saturn's moons and rings	12
Uranus	14
Neptune	16
Grand tour	18
Dwarf planets	20
Glossary	22
Web sites	23
Index	24

The far planets

Eight planets travel around the Sun.
The four closest to the Sun are small worlds.
The four furthest from the Sun are giant planets.

Gas giants

The four planets furthest from the Sun are sometimes called gas giants because they have no solid surface, no land. Instead, they are made mostly of liquid and gas.

Jupiter

SPOTLIGHT ON SPACE

MANY MOONS

The far planets have lots of moons. Jupiter has the most, with more than 65. All four of the far planets have more than 160 moons altogether.

The gas giants are cold worlds because they are so far from the Sun.

Saturn

Uranus

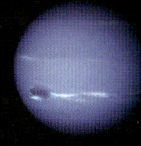

Neptune

THE NINTH PLANET

Until 2006, there was a ninth planet. It was a tiny planet called Pluto. But when more worlds like Pluto were found, astronomers decided to call these small worlds dwarf planets.

Jupiter

If you see a really bright star in the sky at night, it might not be a star at all. It might be the giant planet Jupiter.

Mighty Jupiter

Jupiter is the fifth planet from the Sun and the biggest of all the solar system planets. It's so big that more than 1,300 Earths would fit inside it.

Jupiter's stormy atmosphere is divided into light and dark bands.

Great Red Spot

Lots of storms race around Jupiter. The biggest is called the Great Red Spot. It was seen for the first time more than 300 years ago and it's still there today!

The Great Red Spot is a vast storm bigger than Earth.

SPOTLIGHT ON SPACE

WHAT'S IT MADE OF?

Jupiter is made mostly of hydrogen with some helium and other gases. Under Jupiter's clouds, the gas is squashed so hard that it changes into a liquid.

Exploring Jupiter

In 1610, Italian astronomer Galileo Galilei looked at Jupiter through a telescope and discovered its four biggest moons. In recent years, Jupiter and its moons have been explored by space probes.

Galileo

A spacecraft called *Galileo* spent eight years exploring Jupiter and its moons. It was the fifth spacecraft to visit Jupiter. The first four flew past Jupiter. *Galileo* was the first to orbit it.

Galileo went into orbit around Jupiter on December 8, 1995.

JUPITER'S MOONS

Jupiter's four biggest moons are called Ganymede, Callisto, Io and Europa.

Io

Ganymede

Callisto

Europa

Jupiter's moon Ganymede is the biggest moon in the solar system.

SPOTLIGHT ON SPACE

MINI-PROBE

Galileo dropped a mini-probe into Jupiter's atmosphere. As it fell, it measured the temperature, pressure, and wind speed. It lasted for an hour before it was destroyed by heat and pressure.

Saturn

Saturn is a beautiful golden planet surrounded by broad bright rings. Like Jupiter, it looks like a bright star in the night sky.

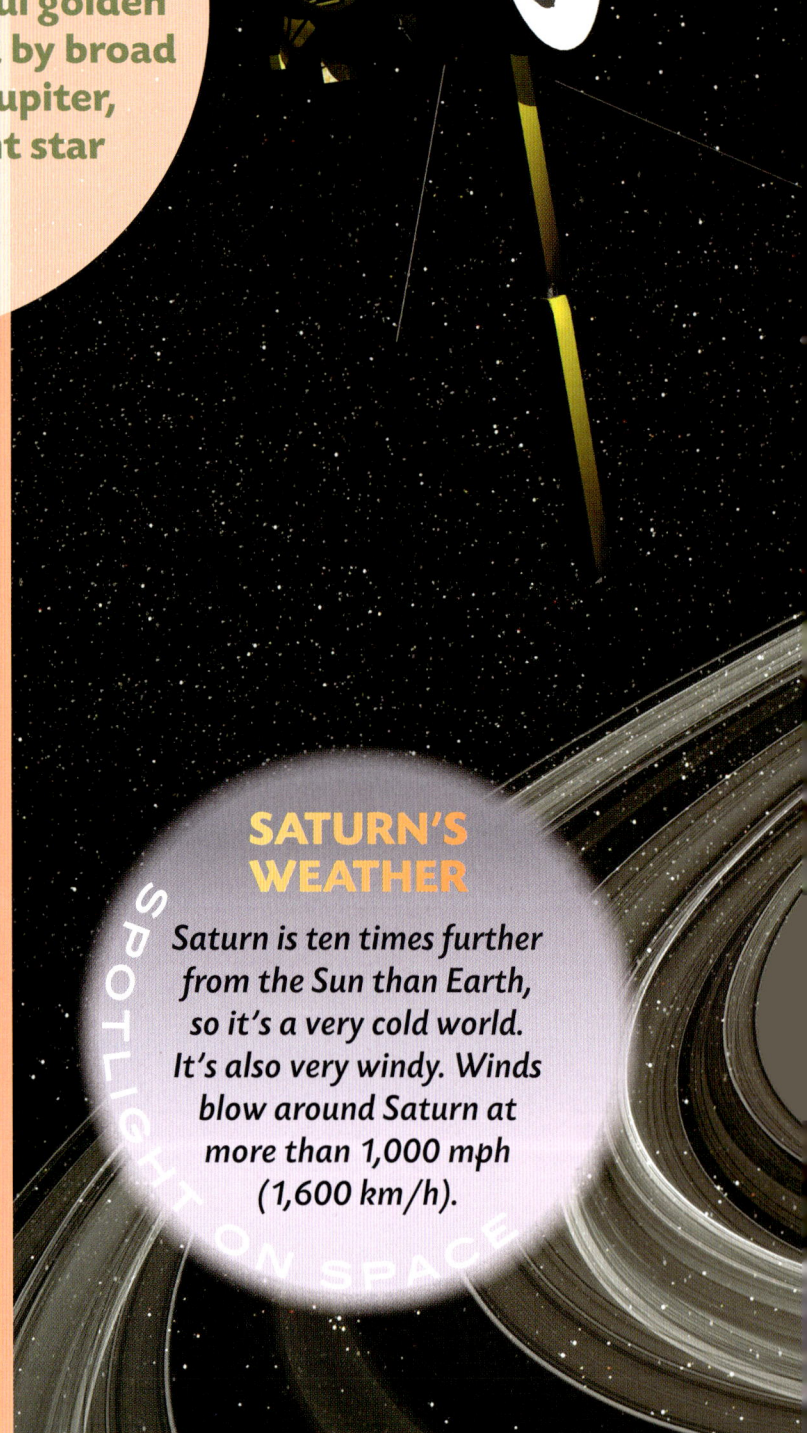

A distant giant

Saturn is not quite as big as Jupiter, but it's still a giant planet. It's made of the same gases as Jupiter; mostly hydrogen with some helium.

SATURN'S WEATHER

Saturn is ten times further from the Sun than Earth, so it's a very cold world. It's also very windy. Winds blow around Saturn at more than 1,000 mph (1,600 km/h).

SPOTLIGHT ON SPACE

Saturn takes 29 Earth years to travel around the Sun.

As Cassini neared Saturn, it fired a rocket to steer it into orbit around the planet.

Mission to Saturn

In 1997 a huge space probe called *Cassini* was sent to explore Saturn and its moons. In 2004 it became the first spacecraft ever to orbit Saturn. And it's still there.

Saturn's moons and rings

Saturn travels through space with dozens of moons and the countless millions of tiny moonlets that make up its rings.

What are the rings made of?
Saturn's rings are made of millions upon millions of pieces of ice with a little added rock. Some pieces are as small as specks of dust. Others are as big as buses.

Saturn's rings are so bright because they reflect sunlight like millions of mirrors.

By 2013, 62 moons had been discovered orbiting Saturn. More will probably be found.

New moons

When the *Cassini* space probe left Earth, Saturn was thought to have 18 moons. *Cassini* discovered another 13. It also found more rings that are too faint to be seen from Earth.

LANDING ON TITAN

Spotlight on space

Cassini dropped a mini-probe called **Huygens** onto one of Saturn's moons, called Titan. *Huygens* found a strange, cold world with a thick orange atmosphere and lakes of liquid methane.

Uranus

Uranus is less than half the size of Jupiter and Saturn, but it's still a gas giant. More than 60 Earths would fit inside it.

Methane gas gives Uranus its blue-green color.

A blue-green world
Uranus is made of the same gases as Jupiter and Saturn—hydrogen and helium—but it has more water, methane and ammonia.

Odd orbit

Uranus orbits the Sun in a very odd way. One of its poles faces the Sun for 42 years and then the other pole faces the Sun for the next 42 years.

Uranus is surrounded by 13 faint rings made of dark dusty particles.

SPOTLIGHT ON SPACE

TELESCOPE DISCOVERY

Uranus was the first planet discovered by using a telescope. The astronomer William Herschel discovered it in 1781. Other astronomers had seen it before, but didn't know it was a planet.

Neptune

Neptune is the smallest and most distant of the four gas giants. It orbits the Sun 30 times further away than Earth and was not discovered until 1846.

Twin world

Neptune is similar to Uranus. Methane in its atmosphere gives it a rich blue color. Neptune has the fastest winds in the solar system, blowing at up to 1,500 mph (2,400 km/h).

Neptune and Uranus are both very cold planets, at about -200°C (-330°F).

ROGUE MOON

Neptune has 14 moons. Triton, its biggest moon, orbits Neptune in the opposite direction to the other moons. It probably formed elsewhere in the solar system and was then captured by Neptune.

GRAVITY TUG

Neptune was discovered by studying Uranus. Astronomers noticed that Uranus was being tugged by another planet's gravity. When they looked for the mystery planet, they found Neptune.

SPOTLIGHT ON SPACE

Neptune's biggest moon, Triton, has volcanoes that spew out nitrogen gas.

GRAND TOUR

Every 175 years, the far planets line up in space. They move into the perfect positions for a space probe to fly past all of them.

Space Voyagers

In 1977, *Voyagers* 1 and 2 were sent on a grand tour of the far planets. *Voyager 1* flew past Jupiter and Saturn. *Voyager 2* flew past all four of the far planets.

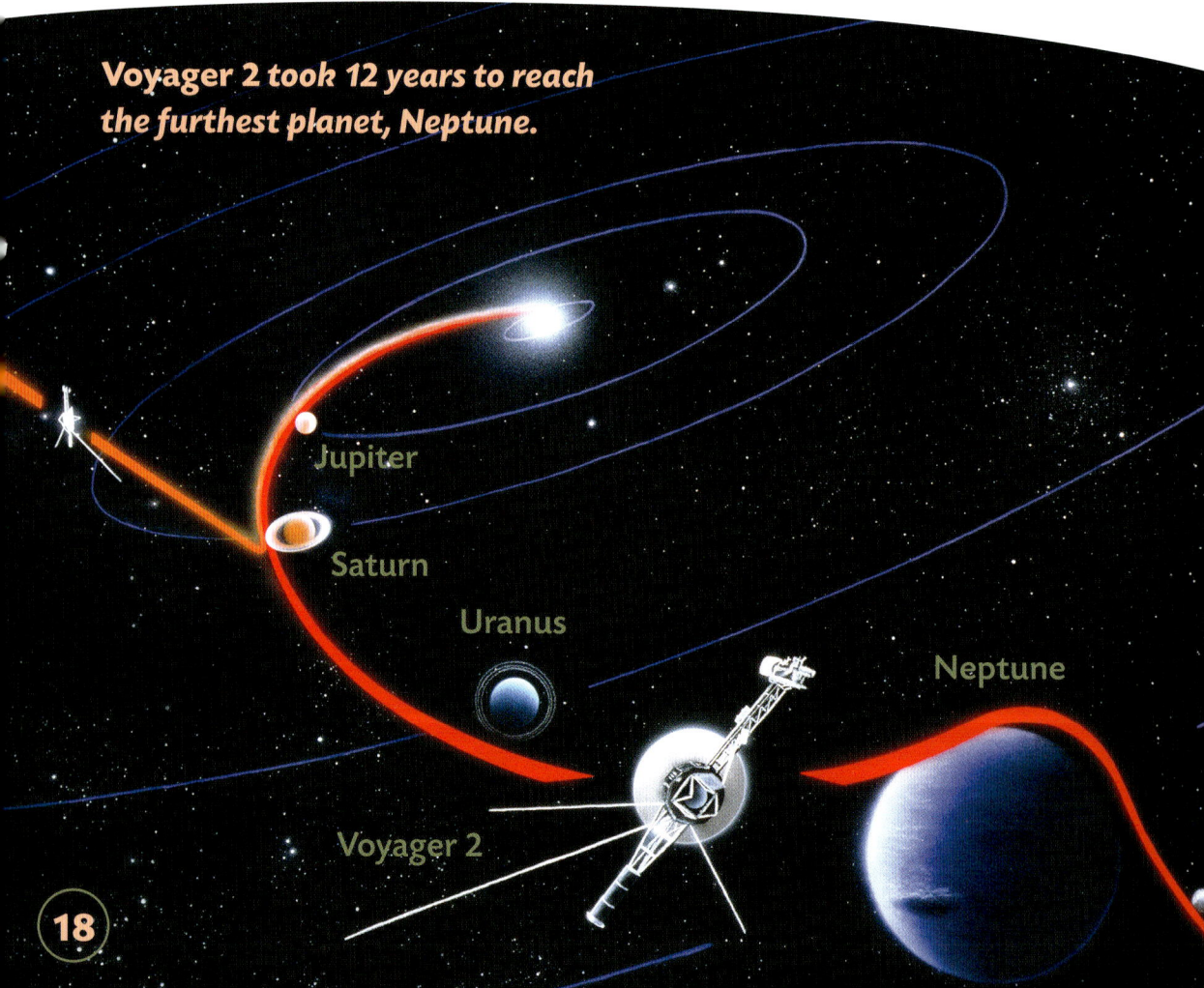

Voyager 2 took 12 years to reach the furthest planet, Neptune.

Jupiter
Saturn
Uranus
Neptune
Voyager 2

The Voyager space probes have a big radio dish to send information to Earth.

Leaving home

In 2013, *Voyager 1* became the first man-made object to leave the solar system. *Voyager 2* will follow it. Their instruments will continue working and sending information to Earth until 2025.

HELLO FROM EARTH

In about 40,000 years, the *Voyager* space probes will fly past stars. Just in case aliens ever find them, both spacecraft carry golden disks with sound recordings from Earth.

Spotlight on space

Dwarf planets

Astronomers have found five small worlds they call dwarf planets. There could be thousands more waiting to be discovered beyond the far planets.

Small worlds

The five dwarf planets found so far are Pluto, Ceres, Eris, Haumea and Makemake. Most of them were found in part of the solar system called the Kuiper Belt.

The Dawn spacecraft on its way to dwarf planet Ceres (right) after visiting asteroid Vesta (left).

Exploring Pluto

A spacecraft called *New Horizons* is on its way to Pluto. It will arrive in 2015 after a nine-year space voyage. *New Horizons* will take the first close-up photographs of Pluto.

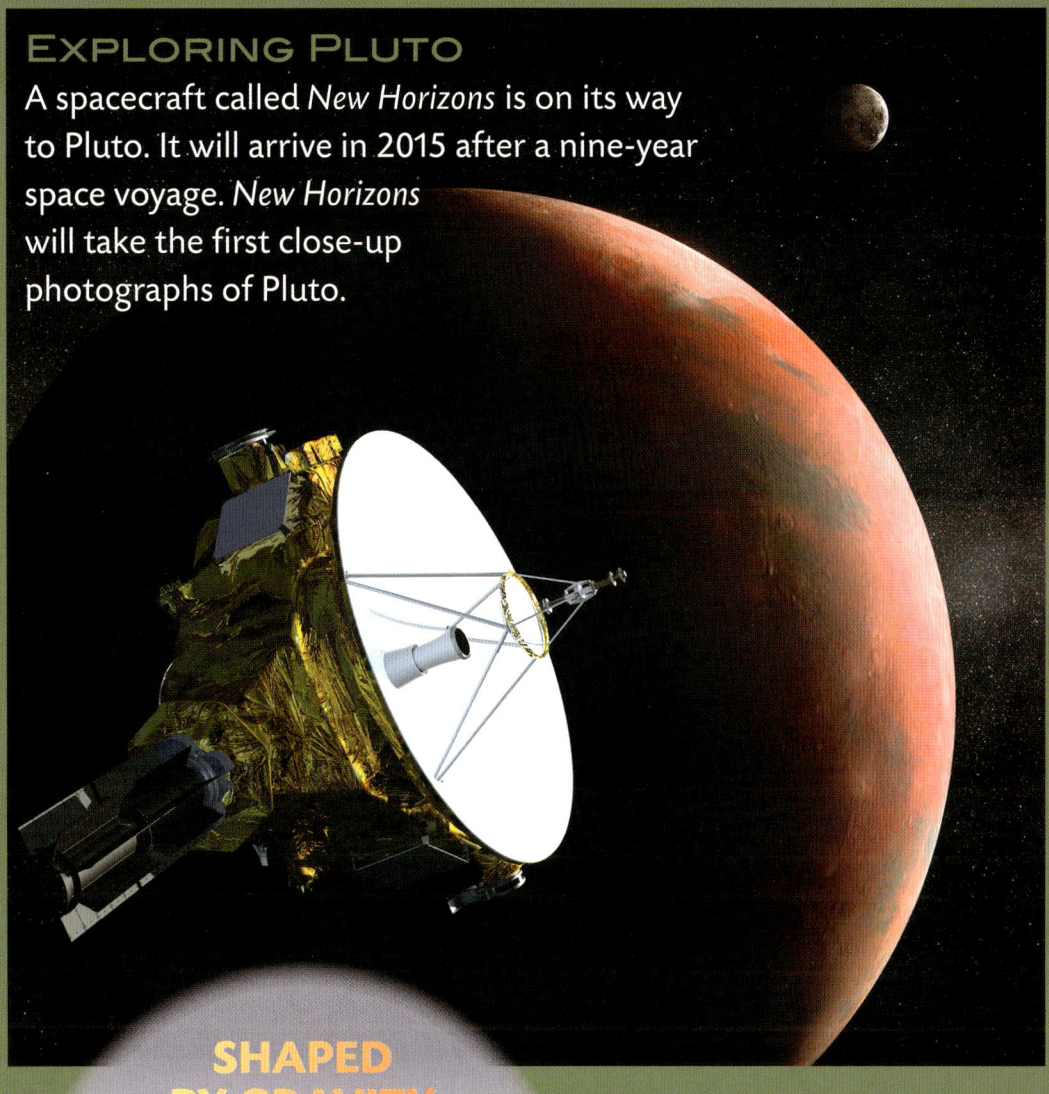

SHAPED BY GRAVITY

To be called a dwarf planet, an object must orbit the Sun and it must be big enough to be pulled into a round shape by its own gravity.

SPOTLIGHT ON SPACE

Five moons orbit Pluto. The biggest, Charon, is half the size of Pluto.

Glossary

ammonia A chemical substance containing nitrogen and hydrogen. Found as a gas on Earth and in the atmospheres of gas giant planets.

astronomer A scientist who studies the Universe beyond Earth.

atmosphere The gases that surround a star, planet, or moon.

dwarf planet An object smaller than a planet that orbits the Sun and is massive enough to be pulled into a round shape by its own gravity.

gas giant A large planet made mainly of gas and liquid.

gravity A force that pulls objects towards each other because of their mass.

helium The second lightest and second most abundant element in the Universe. Helium is found in stars, gas giant planets and, in small amounts, in Earth's atmosphere.

hydrogen The lightest and most abundant element in the Universe. Hydrogen powers stars like the Sun. It's also found in gas giant planets.

Kuiper Belt Part of the solar system beyond the planets where millions of icy worlds including dwarf planets are thought to be.

methane A chemical substance containing carbon and hydrogen. Methane is found in a planet's atmosphere.

moon A small world that orbits another body such as a planet.

orbit The path of a planet, spacecraft, or moon around a larger body.

radio dish A metal bowl that reflects radio waves, often used by spacecraft to send and receive radio signals.

ring Pieces of ice or dust forming a flat disk orbiting a planet. All four gas giant planets are encircled by rings.

solar system The Sun and all the planets, moons, and other bodies that travel through space with it.

space probe An unmanned spacecraft sent from Earth to explore planets, moons and other bodies.

WEB SITES

http://solarsystem.nasa.gov/planets/profile.cfm?Object=Uranus
Lots of facts about Uranus from the American space agency NASA.

http://www.kids.nineplanets.org/uranus.htm
You can read about the strange blue-green world Uranus here.

http://www.ducksters.com/science/neptune.php
Find out how Neptune was discovered and how it compares to Earth.

http://factsforkids.net/neptune-facts-kids/
The top 30 facts about Neptune.

http://kidzone.ws/planets/jupiter.htm
Lots of facts about the giant planet Jupiter.

http://www.sciencekids.co.nz/sciencefacts/planets/jupiter.html
Even more facts about Jupiter.

http://www.esa.int/esaKIDSen/SEMJL6WJD1E_OurUniverse_0.html
Find out more about Saturn, its moons and rings from the European Space Agency.

Index

ammonia 14, 22
astronomers 5, 8, 15, 17, 20, 22

Callisto 9
Cassini 11, 13
Ceres 20
Charon 21

Dawn 20
dwarf planets 5, 20, 21, 22

Earth 6, 7, 10, 13, 14, 16, 19
Europa 9

Galileo 8, 9
Ganymede 9
gases 4, 5, 7, 10, 14, 16, 7
gravity 17, 21, 22

helium 7, 10, 14, 22
Huygens 13
hydrogen 7, 10, 14, 22

Io 9

Jupiter 4, 5, 6, 7, 8, 9, 10, 14, 18

Kuiper Belt 20, 22

methane 13, 14, 16, 22
moons 5, 8, 9, 11, 12, 13, 17, 21, 22

Neptune 5, 16, 17, 18
New Horizons 21
nitrogen 17

orbits 8, 11, 13, 15, 16, 17, 21, 23

Pluto 5, 20, 21

rings 10, 12, 13, 15, 23

Saturn 5, 10, 11, 12, 13, 14, 18
solar system 6, 9, 16, 17, 19, 20, 23
Sun 4, 5, 6, 10, 15, 16, 21

Triton 17

Uranus 5, 14, 15, 16, 17, 18

volcanoes 17
Voyager 1 and *2* 18, 19

winds 9, 10, 16